Benjamin W. Harris

The Annexation Question

Closing argument of B. W. Harris, esq., for the remonstrants against the

annexation of Dorchester to Boston

Benjamin W. Harris

The Annexation Question
Closing argument of B. W. Harris, esq., for the remonstrants against the annexation of Dorchester to Boston

ISBN/EAN: 9783337114398

Printed in Europe, USA, Canada, Australia, Japan

Cover: Foto ©ninafisch / pixelio.de

More available books at **www.hansebooks.com**

THE ANNEXATION QUESTION.

CLOSING ARGUMENT

OF

B. W. HARRIS, ESQ.,

FOR THE REMONSTRANTS AGAINST THE

ANNEXATION OF DORCHESTER TO BOSTON,

BEFORE THE

COMMITTEE ON TOWNS OF THE MASSACHUSETTS LEGISLATURE,

TUESDAY EVENING, APRIL 27, 1869.

BOSTON:
ROCKWELL AND ROLLINS, PRINTERS,
122 WASHINGTON STREET.
1869.

ARGUMENT.

Mr. Chairman and Gentlemen : —

I had hoped to be allowed the privilege, after having made the arrangement, which is certainly not agreeable to any of us, to make the closing argument for the remonstrants in the evening, — I had hoped, I say, to be allowed the privilege of addressing a full committee. Circumstances seem to have interfered to prevent it, and I now enter upon the closing argument in the hope that, if I cannot reach each member of the committee here, there may be some other mode by which the facts which I present and call to their attention may reach them.

I had not the privilege of being present at the first hearing in this case, nor of listening to the opening argument of the learned counsel for the city of Boston ; and the gentleman who appeared here for the petitioners from the town of Dorchester made no opening. I am left, therefore, somewhat to conjecture as to what are the grounds — the main grounds — upon which they propose to rely in the closing argument. I am obliged to take the case as I find it, and to present those considerations which seem to me to bear directly upon the question. I may be obliged to trespass upon your time longer than I should be called upon to do, did I know the grounds really relied upon.

Gentlemen, it is well for us to ask, in the very outstart, what it is which is asked of this Legislature of Massachusetts. WHAT IS ASKED? Upon the record, it is that the town of Dorchester be annexed to the city of Boston ;

and upon the record, which is before us, this is all. But I am told that the learned counsel for the city of Boston announced in his opening that this was but an initiatory step towards annexing to the city of Boston a very large portion of the suburbs, including West Roxbury, Brookline, Brighton, and many other towns. You are not, therefore, merely to decide whether or not it is proper to annex the town of Dorchester to the city of Boston, but you are to remember here that the step now proposed is but the first step in a process which is to extend the city of Boston and its jurisdiction over the strongest, or at least the wealthiest, portion of the Commonwealth. I call your attention to facts and to figures, that we may know precisely what is asked of this Legislature.

The population of the county of Norfolk, by the census of 1865, was 116,306. The population of the city of Roxbury, which has been taken away from the county of Norfolk, was 28,426; and it is now proposed to take from that county the population of the town of Dorchester, — 10,717. These figures are from the census of 1865. The population, of course, has increased greatly since then. But it is proposed by the counsel who appears for the city of Boston to take next, West Roxbury, with a population of 6,912. Next, perhaps, — at least, ultimately, — Brookline, with a population of 5,262. These are the towns to be taken from the county of Norfolk and annexed to the city of Boston, and they reduce the population of the county from 116,306 to 64,989. This, then, upon the single question of population.

Now, sir, as to valuation. By the valuation of 1868, Norfolk county had $82,032,850; Dorchester, $15,326,300; Brookline, $14,870,700; and West Roxbury, $10,302,600; Thus $40,899,600 is to be deducted from a total valuation of $82,032,850. You reduce, then, the valuation of the county of Norfolk to $41,533,250, — a reduction of forty-nine and two-tenths per cent.

But this is what was left of Norfolk county in May, 1868. You must remember that the city of Boston had already taken from the county of Norfolk, by the annexation of Roxbury, a valuation of $26,551,000, as appears by the auditor's report of 1868. You therefore take from the valuation of Norfolk county, if you include Roxbury, $67,450,600, in an entire valuation of $108,583,850, and you reduce it sixty-one and seventy-five one-hundredths per cent.

Mr. TRAIN. — Are you right about that?

Mr. HARRIS. — Precisely right.

Mr. TRAIN. — Your county valuation was made in 1868.

Mr. HARRIS. — I ought to say that I have not been able to get the valuation of Roxbury for 1868, and I have taken its valuation for 1867. If there is any advantage in this, it is upon the side of the petitioners. I believe it has been increased some $2,000,000 by the valuation of 1868.

So much for the effect of this measure upon the wealth and population of the county of Norfolk. Now, let us try the experiment upon the Commonwealth. I think I have taken the towns which are pretty likely to be annexed to the city of Boston, if Dorchester is annexed. Roxbury has been taken. Dorchester is now asked for. In Brookline, agitation is already taking place on this subject, and it is announced here that it is to be taken. West Roxbury, Brighton, (because you must remember that Brighton lies within the embrace of the Charles and Neponset) ; Cambridge, in which agitation has existed upon this subject for some years ; Somerville, that is now knocking at the door of the Legislature, asking for the boon of annexation to the city of Boston ; Chelsea, in which, for aught I know, petitions are circulating to-day, under the stimulus of this measure ; North Chelsea, Winthrop, and Charlestown, the annexation of which last has been a subject of consideration at this very session. By the census of 1865, and the valuation of May 1st, 1868, these towns have a population of 328,247, and a valuation of $618,053,447, which it is proposed to unite under one municipal government.

What is the relation which this population and this wealth

bear to that of the whole Commonwealth? The population of Massachusetts, by the census of 1865, was 1,267,031. The valuation of May, 1868, was $1,220,498,939. By the union of these cities and towns, twenty-six per cent. of the entire population of the Commonwealth, according to the census of 1865, now increased to thirty per cent. by the natural growth of the suburban districts in advance of that of the country, and fifty per cent. and a slight fraction over of the entire wealth of the Commonwealth, will be handed over to the city of Boston. Mr. Chairman and gentlemen, the question was asked here a day or two ago, how much the County Commissioners of Norfolk were going to spend of the public money in meeting this issue? I have in passing only to say, that if the County Commissioners of Norfolk should sit by and see this dismemberment of the old county go on without resistance, they would meet the merited contempt and scorn of every citizen of the county who did not happen to be an annexationist. Their duty is plain, and they are here attempting to discharge that duty through myself as their humble instrument.

When the city of Roxbury was annexed to Boston, the distinguished gentleman at the head of the committee who reported the bill undertook to soften and mitigate the blow in his report to the Legislature by these words: "The county of Norfolk, of which Roxbury is a part, can suffer no real injury by the union. With her territory joining the united cities, her prospect and advantage for rapid increase in the future will be equal to any county in the State." The chairman of that committee appears here to-day, asking that you further dismember the county of Norfolk by taking from it three of the largest and fairest towns, not only of the county, but I might almost say of the Commonwealth itself. These words imported a promise that, when Roxbury was taken, the fair prospect of Norfolk for future growth should be left untouched by the Legislature for a period at least of more than two years.

Having seen what is asked by these petitioners, permit me for a few moments to inquire who ask it, and how it is asked.

In the first place, the city of Boston asks it. No, sir, the City Council of Boston ask it. Mark you, sir, that not one single man in this whole great city of Boston, who is not an office-holder under it, has been before you, either by petition or in testimony, to say that there is any necessity on the part of Boston for this scheme of annexation. The City Council of Boston, — and the City Council of Boston are supposed to know what they want, and why they want it, — on the 10th day of December, 1868, deliberately and solemnly, in the presence, I have no doubt, of my brother Train, perhaps actuated and moved by him, aided and assisted by that " intelligent committee " of Dorchester, who stood behind and assisted him, passed this order, giving the reasons for annexation : —

" *Whereas*, in the opinion of the City Council, it has become necessary, in order to complete the systems of drainage and harbor improvements which have been devised for the benefit of Boston by the various commissioners who have had and now have these subjects in charge, to annex a portion or the whole of the town of Dorchester to the city of Boston, —

" *Ordered*, That His Honor the Mayor be requested to appoint a commission of three discreet and intelligent persons, who shall carefully examine the subject, in all its financial, industrial, and sanitary relations, cause such surveys to be made by the city surveyor, or under his direction, as they may consider necessary, and report the result of their doings, with such suggestions as they may think proper, to the city council, as soon as may be."

I shall have the honor, before I close, to try the reason assigned in this order by the testimony. I say the City Council alone ; and we are not so familiar with the secrets of the City Hall as to know how this happened to emanate from the City Council of Boston at precisely this period. We know this, however : that the City Council has not been supported and sustained by the written petition of a single resident or citizen of Boston.

The petition from Boston is in accordance with this general order passed by the city government in April, 1866 : —

" *Ordered.* That whenever the City Council or Selectmen of any city or town, whose territory adjoins that of the city of Boston, shall notify the City Council of Boston, that in accordance with a vote of their respective bodies they are empowered to consult with the authorities of Boston with a view to the annexation to the city of Boston of their city or town, it shall be the duty of His Honor, the Mayor of Boston, to appoint three commissioners from the citizens of Boston to meet an equal number from the city or town making the request."

I suppose the order which was adopted on the tenth of December, 1868, was in compliance with this general policy, that Boston shall take advantage of every apparent inclination on the part of any city or town to become a part of this city, and reach out its arms, appoint its commissioners, and see if it cannot find some reason under heaven why it should come in and subject itself to the city government of Boston. But I will not dwell longer upon that subject.

It is said that here are 860 names on the petition from the town of Dorchester. I have not counted them, but I believe the reckoning makes them fall short a little. Throwing off thirty-one names which happen to be written two or three times, and allowing for such inadvertent inaccuracies, which cannot but happen in such cases, you have about 829 names. The petition is labelled upon the back, " 860 legal voters of the town of Dorchester." We have shown that 233 of the names are not legal voters of the town of Dorchester. It is reduced, then, to 596. I will not undertake to be exactly accurate upon that point.

Now, how were these names obtained, and what influenced the petition? Let us find out whether the 829 or 596 of the inhabitants of Dorchester, whose names appear on this petition, so artfully worded, really desire annexation. They want *the whole of Dorchester annexed*, according to the petition. The only word in capitals in the heading of that petition is the word "WHOLE." And why should such a petition come here? It is perfectly easy to explain it, sir. A line, which one of our humorous citizens of Dorchester has characterized as a "wheelbarrow line," was run through the town from the Roxbury line up to the centre of the town, setting the town-house upon one side, and the church upon the other, and running over to Granite Bridge. The people of Dorchester, remembering their glorious history, clinging to the associations of the past, loving the dear, good old town, immediately arose and cried out, "The whole or none!" and that cry was echoed through every district, and every portion of the town of Dorchester. A hired messenger travelled through the town with a petition praying for the annexation of the WHOLE of Dorchester; and he got 829 names, 233 of which are neither voters, nor, so far as we know, residents. "The whole or none." We have had here, to-day, gentlemen who say that they signed that petition upon the statement that that was its object. I would not undertake to say, Mr. Chairman, that there are not the names of a great many men upon that petition who desire annexation; but I do maintain that there are many, very many, there, who, upon the *naked* question of annexation, will say No! Let us, then, not give to that petition the weight which is claimed for it, but give to it just the weight, if we can, to which it is entitled. This was a canvass, mark you, Mr. Chairman, in which the person canvassing, says, "We don't want Dorchester divided; but if they are going to take a portion, let them take the whole!"

You must remember, too, that the impression had gone out, and become quite common in the community, that a portion of the town of Dorchester must be taken, on account of the demands for sanitary purposes of the city of Boston. Mr. A. A. Childs came here this morning, and told us he signed it because he believed that the city of Boston must have it for sanitary purposes, and he desired to benefit the city of Boston. He went to the town meeting, and heard the beautiful orations which were there delivered; he heard the

2

descriptions of the wharves lining the whole shore from Milton Lower Mills, along Dorchester Bay, clear round South Boston Point, and up to the Hartford & Erie Railroad station, which annexation is expected to create. We all know how much of fiction, and how little of real fact, " Oliver Optic " can put into any book which he writes. Those of us who happened to hear that oration know precisely how much of fiction, and how much of fact, was given on that occasion, to interest, amuse, and delight the audience assembled in the town hall on that day. But Mr. Childs came away from the meeting, satisfied that nothing had been shown which indicated that Boston wanted any portion of the town of Dorchester for sanitary purposes; and he comes here to-day, and tells you that he don't see any reason under heaven why Dorchester should be wanted by Boston.

Now we come to another point, — the action of the town meeting. They say there were 544 voters in favor of annexation to 62 opposed. Mark you, again, the mode in which the matter is carried through the town meeting. Upon the question of appointing a committee to resist annexation, the vote stood two to one, — two opposed to the appointment of that committee, to one in favor of it. You may ask me, " Where are your remonstrants?" I say to you, even in that meeting, got up under circumstances so peculiar, — even in that meeting, upon a fair and square vote, one-third of the population resisted it. But Mr. Micah Dyer, Jr., with his accustomed shrewdness, gets up in the town meeting, and introduces this order : —

"That the moderator of the meeting appoint a committee of fifteen *to oppose any division of the town of Dorchester*, and to advocate the annexation of the *whole* town to the city of Boston before the Legislature at its present session."

Here we have it again : *No division of the town!* And on that vote, even Mr. Thomas Temple, an opponent of annexation, among others, voted *Yea*. I say to you, Mr. Chairman and gentlemen, when you count upon 544 voters in that meeting in favor of annexation, you mistake. The town of Dorchester has not had a full discussion of this matter. But I have a word to say about that town meeting. I do not wish to be severe upon anybody; I do not mean to utter a word which may be considered personal. But I have had occasion in the course of this investigation to animadvert somewhat upon the conduct of the chairman of that meeting. It did seem to me that Mr. Upham, who was last year the chairman of the committee chosen to oppose annexation, but who happens to be, this year, a convert to annexation, — it did seem to me a little strange that under his management fair play could not have been a little better secured. It did seem, I thought, that, where a majority of the committee opposed to annexation, of which he was chairman, had a written report ready to present to the meeting, Mr. Upham did not do quite the fair thing in reading a report signed by himself as chairman, and having it acted upon before the majority of the committee could get a chance to make it known that they had a report ready, and he the chairman of the meeting too. I thought then, and think now, he did not give the opponents of this measure quite a fair chance. But this is, after all, of very little consequence.

This petition and this vote were very much influenced by the cry that had gone abroad in the town, and which had made an impression upon many people, "that a portion of the town must inevitably be surrendered to Boston for sanitary reasons." Whether that cry had any foundation in fact, we will see by and by.

But how was that meeting constituted? Mr. Putnam, who runs a large nail factory, hires two four-horse wagons, and hires 42 voters to go and vote for annexation. My brother Train may object to the statement in that form, and I will state just what he did. He had 42 voters in his employ who would vote in favor of annexation, and he said, "Boys, I will pay you your wages, nothing shall be deducted from your day's labor, and I will pay your transportation up and back, if you will go and vote for annexation ;" and they went. It is a very easy way to carry a town meeting, if you only have men enough in your employ. Now *proper* efforts to get out voters are perfectly legitimate. Nobody objects to them ; but when one wants a half-inch pipe from the water-works in Boston carried to his factory; for the purpose of supplying water for his steam-engine, it is not quite right to hire voters and transport them to the polls, and then claim that a majority so obtained is indicative of public sentiment. I rather question the integrity of such efforts to get votes in a matter of this nature.

Mr. Temple comes in here, and tells you that another element entered into this question ; that a certain portion of the community who believe in selling rum, under the excellent administration of Mr. Pope and Mr. Upham, while the old liquor law was in force, were obliged to shut up shop and take down their signs : and in his neighborhood it was said by this class of people, "Let us go to Boston, and then the d—d State constables can't reach us." How far that had any influence, I don't know. It may be that it did not influence many votes ; but it seems to me that it is a matter for your consideration.

I make these comments that you may understand that all this show is not quite substantial ; that there is a little something here which may well be scrutinized.

Why, gentlemen, Hon. Marshall P. Wilder, a man of very general reputation in Massachusetts, who has stood up in Dorchester town meetings for forty years, or ought to have done so, was not known in that meeting, it is said. They did not respect his gray hairs, and they hissed him and hooted him, at first, although he came to speak on their own side. They were not the substantial men of the town of Dorchester who came there to vote. Not that I would say that there were not many of the very best citizens of Dorchester in that meeting ; the wealthiest, the most intelligent, if you please, — men whom I highly respect, — advocating annexation; but what I mean to say is, that there were some others there, new to the place, and influenced by other considerations than the welfare either of Dorchester or Boston. The meeting was noisy, and not such as we should expect in that town. Mr. Loring comes and tells you that he could not be heard; that fair play could not be had. Dr. Jarvis was able to speak for a few minutes, and Mr. Drew was able to speak for half an hour or so; but the rest of the time occupied by the opponents of annexation was very short; while, on the other side, we had a splendid oration from our friend Oliver Optic; we had an oration of a few moments from Mr. Marshall P. Wilder, after his own friends would let him speak; and we had orations from other persons.

There were several eloquent speeches, in which we had magnificent parks described, and all those fine things, that were to rise immediately upon the annexation to Boston; and the people were carried away captive by the eloquence of these gentlemen, and they finally voted, 544 to 62, that upon their consciences *they were opposed to any division of the town of Dorchester*, — for that is the substance of the whole thing. There were in that meeting wealthy landholders, looking for a rise; and poor laborers, looking for jobs; the extremes met.

I will say no more upon the subject of that meeting. I only ask you to consider that these petitions, whether from the city of Boston or the town of Dorchester, are not petitions and prayers representing, as they purport to do, the real sentiment of the community. They may to some extent represent, but they certainly are not the best indications of, the sentiment of the town of Dorchester.

We had some altercation between the witnesses as to what took place at that town meeting. Mr. Loring thinks he was abused there, and that he has been abused, misrepresented, and entirely misunderstood here. Mr. Peirce came in here to-day and said — and it was echoed by Mr. Clark — that Mr. Loring, upon that occasion, made a speech that people should laugh at; that he shook a certain document at the people of the town, and told them if they knew what was in it, they would vote against annexation. I propose to show you, before I get through, what is in that document, — the Report of the Auditor of Boston, — for it may influence you, if it did not them. Mr. Loring is not a man to be silenced when he thinks he is right, here or there. He can point to as honorable a record as any witness who has appeared before you. It is as clean as that of any man who speaks against him. In integrity, in patriotism, in high honor, no man who has appeared here, upon either side of the question, is his superior. And many persons who have appeared here are of the very highest character and standing in the community.

Mr. Chairman, it may be said, because it is an old argument upon such occasions, that if annexation is *not* wanted by the town of Dorchester, there is no harm in reporting a bill. That may or may not be so; but I apprehend I address a committee this evening who are not prepared to evade the responsibility which the Legislature has thrown upon them. You are not to leave a great question of State policy, a great question affecting the rights and interests of the people of the Commonwealth, to a town meeting, even in Dorchester. The responsibility is upon you, Mr. Chairman and gentlemen, to decide that there is here an *emergency* and a call for the act which is sought to be passed. That, I think, is all I need to say on this branch of the subject.

Now, sir, coming nearer to the point in hand, what proof will you require before you will grant the prayer of the petitioners and give them a bill? I am aware that I am somewhat out of place before a committee of the Legislature, and not exactly accustomed to the modes of procedure in such cases. I think some gentlemen upon the committee may understand and appreciate my position. In a court of law, in a tribunal where evidence is admitted under settled rules, I should know better what would be required. I apprehend, however, that you will not make it widely different. In a case affecting so great interests as this, I think you will require of these petitioners, that they show by testimony, not by argument, not by words outside of your chamber, not by insinuation or innuendo, not by mere figures of speech, that a *public necessity* exists for the measure they ask for. Nothing less, it seems to me, ought to be required.

SEWERAGE.

They have said — and it will figure somewhat in this case, I suppose — that some portion of the territory of Dorchester is needed by the city of Boston for the purposes of sewerage. Let me advert briefly to the position which this subject occupies before you. Not a single witness, not one solitary witness has been called before you to prove that any necessity exists for the annexation of any portion of the territory of Dorchester for the purposes of sewerage, either of Roxbury or Boston. Not only that, but we have the testimony on our part of Hon. Josiah Quincy, who came in this morning, and told you that every foot of land which is required for sewerage purposes, lies now within the exclusive jurisdiction of the city of Boston. Neither my brother Train, nor his friend Mr. Bowerman, has dared to bring a man before this committee to show that there is, at present, any drain or sewer contemplated. Where is your city surveyor with his plans? Where is the evidence that at any future time it will become necessary to drain through the territory of Dorchester? Mr. Quincy doubts whether Stony Brook, in Roxbury, can ever be successfully drained through the territory of Dorchester, so as to empty the sewerage of that city into Dorchester Bay. Not a word from my brother, not a word from the petitioners of Dorchester, not a syllable from any source upon the subject of drainage! And yet that is the theory upon which they started. They said they must have some portion of Dorchester, to carry out the great scheme of sewerage which the present and former commissioners had laid out. Let us see what the Board of Harbor Commissioners say in the report annexed to this city document, No. 28, for the year 1869 : —

"COMMONWEALTH OF MASSACHUSETTS.

"HARBOR COMMISSIONERS' OFFICE, CITY HALL,
"Boston, Feb. 25, 1869.

"HON. CHARLES R. TRAIN, *Chairman Commissioners on the annexation of Dorchester to Boston :* —

"SIR, — The Board of Harbor Commissioners have the honor to make the following report upon the request of the Commissioners appointed by the Mayor of Boston to consider the subject of the annexation of a portion or the whole of the town of Dorchester to the city of Boston : —

"*Upon the general question of the expediency of enlarging the water front of the city, it would not be proper for this Board to express any opinion, as they have jurisdiction equally over the water fronts of Boston and Dorchester, and can take as efficient measures for the protection of navigation and the preservation of the harbor, whether the corporation limits are diminished or enlarged.*

"In regard to the matter of drainage, the Commissioners, desirous of furnishing such information as they could command, directed their engineer to examine into the subject of deflecting the drainage of Stony Brook from Charles River to Dorchester Bay. The results of his examinations have been communicated to the Board, as follows : —

"The topography of the country, of which Stony Brook is the natural drain, does not admit of other relief for its water-shed, except at points near the mouth of said brook, at is confluence with Muddy River.

"Between this general locality and the shores of Dorchester Bay the ground is low and level, and a drain or sewer carrying even a part of the flowage of Stony Brook, at times of freshet, would have to be of large capacity, and through expensive ground to occupy for this purpose.

"The distance from the nearest point of Stony Brook. favorable for deflecting drainage, to the present nearest shore of Dorchester Bay, is about two miles, — 10,500 feet.

"The distance from the same point to Charles River is about one and a quarter miles, — 6,500 feet.

"*The route most favorable and practical for a drain or sewer, turning Stony Brook into Dorchester Bay, passes just tangent to the township line of Dorchester, and is already within the limits of the city of Boston, near the head-waters of South Bay, and would not, therefore, involve questions of municipal interest.*

"The physical bearing of the drainage from Stony Brook is a questionable one. As a tributary to Charles River it is of value. Its volume, during a recent freshet was 400 cubic feet per second. The deposits from it as a sewer would be injurious; but its influences in comparison with the water volume of Charles River, or with its mud deposits, are of small proportion.

"Respectfully submitted,

"JOSIAH QUINCY,

"*Chairman Board of Harbor Commissioners.*"

The very first page of the book opens with the pretence that something must be done to complete the system of drainage, and that Dorchester territory is needed for that purpose; and the last page gives an entire and complete refutation of the whole pretence. There is not to be found in the city of Boston a man who dares stand before the committee, and say that at present, or in the future, an inch of the territory of Dorchester is required for the purposes of sewerage.

THE HARBORS AND RIVERS.

Then comes the subject of harbor and river improvements, which was also put into that order. It is met in precisely the same way. It is sustained by precisely the same testimony. I do not know what was said in the opening; I do not know what may be said in the closing; but I know this, that I have a right to stand before a committee of the Legislature and demand that when a reason of that kind is pressed upon them it shall stand upon some proofs, from some source. Gentlemen, be not deceived by talk about river and harbor improvements, when His Honor the Mayor, when the learned counsel, himself a member of the City Government, when the Auditor, the two Assessors, and one Alderman, who have been here, have neither of them dared to open their lips upon the subject of harbor and river improvements. It is met by Mr. Quincy, who upon that subject makes a reply, in the second paragraph of the report which I have just read, that is quite conclusive.

3

I think I may now dismiss these two subjects, which made the substance of this order. The city of Boston started off with a pretence upon the subject of drainage and sewerage and harbor and river improvements, which is openly abandoned before a committee of the Legislature.

Now, sir, how stands the matter? A learned Commission was appointed. The old reasons were abandoned, some new ones must be had, and the Commission sought to hunt them up. We will see whether they have succeeded. These two pet reasons are gone, and I shall not again advert to them directly, although I may have occasion incidentally to refer to them.

HIGHWAYS AND STREETS.

You will find in that report, and you will hear it outside of this room, if not here, that the city of Boston requires some of the territory of Dorchester for the purpose of extending its highways and streets into the country. The city of Boston wants jurisdiction over Dorchester for the purpose of making broader avenues. Very well. That is a statement which, if true, ought to receive the utmost consideration from this committee. But, Mr. Chairman, no man has been brought here to say to you that there is a single street contemplated in the plans of any surveyor, or agitated before any board, whether of the city of Boston, or the city of Roxbury, or the county of Norfolk. There is not an avenue asked for or contemplated from the territory of Boston into the territory of Dorchester, or even dreamed of in the imagination of the wildest of these annexationists. Oh, yes! I do His Honor the Mayor great injustice. He did say, that some time in the far future it might become necessary to build a road from South Boston to Roxbury, and that a small piece of the territory of Dorchester would become desirable for that purpose. South Bay is unfilled; hundreds of acres, for aught I know, of unfilled land are now lying between South Boston and Roxbury, and yet possibly in the future there may be a road built over that South Bay into Roxbury, or that vicinity; and when that emergency comes, the County Commissioners of the county of Norfolk will do as they always have done, open a highway for the people of the city of Boston, and see that it is properly built.

Is there anything more upon the subject of highways? Have you heard anything more in this room upon the subject of highways now needed? The streets of Dorchester are as good as those of any other town in the Commonwealth. There is one broad avenue which you had the pleasure or discomfort of riding over, called Dorchester Avenue, upon which there is a vast amount of travel, no doubt, from Quincy, and those towns beyond, through which a horse-railroad passes, and it meets, and is a continuation of Federal Street, in Boston. It is said that this street ought really to be in the hands of the city of Boston, because they would spend $25,000 upon it. Well, I do not know but they would; but, in passing down Federal Street, I have noticed that, at least, one-half mile of the same road, extending from Dorchester line into the very heart of the city, is in a worse condition to-day than Dorchester Avenue ever has been in the past. Why not build up to your line, gentlemen of Boston, who are so anxious for a little more territory? Why not fill up your city? Why not build and finish this street up to the Dorchester line? Show them by contrast what they ought to do, and I assure you the people of Dorchester will do it.

Is there anything else upon the subject of highways which ought to engage your attention, and which ought to be considered by you as rendering the annexation of Dorchester to Boston necessary? I apprehend not, and, therefore, I dismiss this branch of the subject.

SCHOOLS.

They say there is some little difficulty about schools. Upon the subject of schools I propose to put the town of Dorchester in comparison with the city of Boston. I say that Boston does not do her duty in the education of the youth within her borders better than Dorchester, and I prove it by the report of the Board of Education. By that report, just published, it is shown that the amount appropriated for each child, from five to fifteen years of age, is as follows: Brookline, the best town in the State, appropriates $29.82½. Boston stands the sixth municipality upon the list, and appropriates 17.71_{10}^{9}$. Dorchester, the seventh town in the State, appropriates 17.62_{10}^{8}$. Upon this point, the city of Boston, with its immense wealth, is just nine cents and one mill ahead of the town of Dorchester. But this does not justly show the rank of Boston upon the subject of schools. Dorchester stands 113 upon the list of appropriations, — not the highest, but 113, — while Boston stands 30´. I speak now of the appropriation as compared with the assessed wealth. Dorchester appropriates 3_{10}^{7}$ mills per cent., and Boston 1_{10}^{7}$. Now, sir, when the people of Dorchester assess themselves twice as much, according to their valuation, as the city of Boston does, for school purposes, as shown by public documents, I think it is an answer to those people who say that the schools of Dorchester are not what they should be.

But I do not find fault with Boston in this particular. Boston is a magnificent city in all these respects. Boston stands at the head of the continent for liberality for all the purposes of education and charity, — stands, not only, perhaps, ahead of any other city of this country, but almost of the world. We love to praise and applaud Boston; but it is the happiness of the people of Dorchester to be able to point to a record upon this subject quite as fair, quite as brilliant and honorable.

Upon the score of attendance on the public schools, Dorchester stands 98 upon the list, and her attendance is 82: 51 per cent. Boston stands 222, — away down the list, — with an attendance of 72. 28 per cent.

Boston has appropriated for the school buildings of the city one-half of one per cent., and Dorchester nine-tenths of one per cent., upon its valuation. You saw, Mr. Chairman, away out in the woods, at Matapan, one of those new school-houses, just erected by the liberality of the town of Dorchester. I have no doubt it attracted your attention. Away out there in the woods you saw a new school-house just finished, at an expense of from $30,000 to $40,000. And yet, some gentlemen speak lightly about the schools of Dorchester! They would like the advantages of the Boston Latin School. Yes, and Mr. May, Chairman of the School Committee of Dorchester, an honorable, upright, and high-minded man, talks a little about the Latin School; and yet, out there in town meeting the other day, he got up and urged an appropriation of $50,000 for a High School in Dorchester,—a school where the Latin language, and the Greek language, and all the modern languages are to be taught; and he urged it upon the people of Dorchester upon this ground, *that if they were annexed to Boston, they might not be able to get that school, or a branch of the Latin School, but if they built it now they would have it.* And the town voted it, — $50,000 for a High School in Dorchester, — as he desired, and as they ought.

POLICE.

Some of our fanciful and imaginative friends have talked about the police system of the town of Dorchester. Mr. Upham is extremely anxious to have the police system of Boston. He has been chairman of the Board of Selectmen for six or seven years, and $1,700 are the highest figures ever reached for the police. When Mr. Pope and himself were enforcing the liquor law in the town of Dorchester (and I can bear testimony to their efficiency and faithfulness in that regard), they closed the hotels and the rum-shops at an expense of only $700. 380 warrants were issued in two years and a half by the chief magistrate of that region, as I may call him, for there is nobody else who undertakes to act in that capacity but Mr. Temple, — including all that came from Randolph and other portions of the Commonwealth. The police record of the town of Dorchester will not half equal in the number of arrests that of the town of Randolph, a little further back in the country. Police force indeed! $8,000 appropriated this very year for a police force in the town of Dorchester, where they never spent $2,000 a year!. We seldom hear of a robbery or burglary out in Dorchester. It is a quiet, peaceful, and orderly town, as everybody must admit. Yet Mr. Upham thinks, upon the whole, he would like a little more police. He is ambitious to come in under the direction of the Boston police. It may be a matter of taste with him. I differ in taste. Perhaps, sir, this is all it is best to say upon the police system of Boston, until the Legislature get through with the subject.

Mr. Mears comes in and tells us they had a riot in Neponset some five or six years ago, and wanted more policemen, and they sent into Boston and got forty-five. They say Mr. Putnam's men refused to work without an increase of wages; they wanted ninepence or a shilling more, and wouldn't work. They got together, had a band of music, paraded through the streets, and had a good deal of fun, and refused to go to work for Mr. Putnam until he would give them higher wages. Mr. Putnam and his friends wanted to find some law by which these men could be compelled to go to work, and they rushed into Boston and got forty-five policemen, took them out there, and they arrested twelve of the men, and brought them up before the Superior Court of the county of Norfolk; but they were all discharged because they had committed no crime. The Dorchester police knew what crime was, and they made a discrimination. They knew enough to know that they had no business to arrest a man who struck for higher wages. That is the substance and whole amount of his testimony. There was disturbance and noise; there were some things done which

nobody would countenance or approve; but are you prepared to say, gentleman, that, because Mr. Putnam could
not keep his workmen at his own price, the town of Dorchester shall be annihilated?

SIDEWALKS.

Something has been said about sidewalks. I have not
much to say about that, for I do not believe that the fact
that the people out in Dorchester want to build sidewalks
and pay for them, as the people of Boston do, is any good
reason for annexation. But if you will look at Chap. 48 of
the General Statutes, you will find that the town authorities
of Dorchester have a right to lay out sidewalks and assess
one-half the cost upon the abutter. The city of Boston
makes the landholder pay half the cost of his sidewalk.
Gentlemen, the same thing can be done in Dorchester. The
fact is, the people of Dorchester have been misled into
believing that, if they can only get annexed to Boston, the
city will give them streets and sidewalks, and not charge
them a cent. But the law of the Commonwealth is quite
the reverse. They will have to pay precisely as they do in
Boston.

SURFACE DRAINAGE.

Hard pushed for reasons in favor of annexation, Mr.
Upham at last finds one which satisfies him. He has seen
Judge Leland! It also occurs to him that a little surface
drainage is needed in Dorchester.

Gentlemen, where is there any surface drainage needed
which the town of Dorchester cannot furnish? Mr. J. H.
Robinson, a gentleman who is an annexationist, was called
by me, you remember. He has a little land lying down upon
the Roxbury line, where the bottom is solid rock. It is just
a little over the line, and he has got it pretty clearly in
his head, — and I justify him entirely, — that if Dorchester was annexed to Boston, possibly there might be water

enough in the reservoir on Chestnut Hill to enable Boston to extend a pipe out over his rocky bottom and give him water, and save him the expense of wells. He thinks, in that particular, annexation would be a blessing to him; he says so. I agree with him. I have no doubt about it. But what does Mr. Robinson tell us with regard to the drainage of Dorchester? He tells us that Dorchester can take care of herself. She has no surface drainage which she cannot well provide for. It is hill and dale; it is not a flat country; it is a well-drained town; it has plenty of water, except in one or two places; and, like a fair and honest man, he comes up here and tells us, that, though opposed to us for certain reasons of the pocket, yet all this talk about surface drainage, in his judgment, is foolish and absurd. I am very much obliged to Mr. J. H. Robinson. I think he appears very well in contrast with our friend, the chairman.

BOSTON WANTS ROOM.

But, Mr. Chairman and gentlemen, there are, it is claimed, other and graver reasons, why Dorchester should surrender her corporate existence, and become a part of the city of Boston. "Boston wants room; Boston has not room for her middle classes; Boston should be allowed to extend into the country, to find cheap land for her people; Boston is full." Two years ago Boston was full, and you took 1,500 acres of unoccupied land in Roxbury to supply the demand. Boston is full again, and she will be full, just as long as there is an acre of land outside of her that her avaricious eyes may covet. Boston, it is said, must have room to extend; and we have had some evidence that the people on Fort Hill, — 185 families, 3,000 people, — and in Church Street, — 867 families, 3,520 people, — have got to move. No suggestion is made, and so I make it, that Fort Hill is only being cut down, and Church Street is only being raised up, and that the territory is precisely the same as before. But they say Fort Hill is to be used for warehouses. Church Street is not to be used for warehouses for the present generation, but it is to be occupied by respectable men of the middle class until the property rises, as it may in the future, so high that it must be used for more expensive buildings. The Lowell depot is to be changed, they say, and 719 families, 3,043 people, are to be driven out of that territory. They want to colonize these people, I suppose, in the town of Dorchester. An enviable and most desirable colony would undoubtedly migrate from Fort Hill into the beautiful suburbs of Dorchester; they would cluster around that grand park of 800 acres, of which I doubt not we shall have a poetic description from my brother Train, because we know he has a fine and vivid imagination. But what are the facts? Do not let us be deceived upon a question of this magnitude. When the annexation of the city of Roxbury was upon the carpet, the city of Boston found it necessary to call for some information from the President of the Water Board, and he made a report, which is dated "City Hall, Feb. 18, 1867." You may have seen it, Mr. Chairman, but I beg leave to read a portion of it, because it is something which I think the city of Boston cannot controvert, and will not attempt to here. They talk about the want of vacant land; but they have not put a witness on the stand who has sworn that there was not vacant land in Boston. East Boston has it, South Boston has it, the Back Bay lands are unfilled, and there are unoccupied flats all around us, capable of increasing, to a large extent, the available territory within the city. But, gentlemen, I have the figures : —

The area of Boston proper (not including streets) is about . . 970 acres.
Of this there are built upon and improved about . . . . . 630 "
Leaving of available unimproved land about . . . . 340 "
The filled area of East Boston (not including streets and
  squares) is about . . . . 660 "
Of this there are built upon and improved about . . . . . 170 "

"But," says some gentleman, "East Boston has no ferry; East Boston has no bridge." Yes, but when we go to

4

New York, and look across the river to Brooklyn, we see thousands of boats, almost, plying between the two cities, transporting thousands and tens of thousands of people from New York to that beautiful city across the water. Ferries are there, — and why? Simply because the population of New York is so great that they need an outlet, and they have ferries, and sustain them; and when Boston is full, you will find no difficulty of communication between East Boston and the city. When Boston is really full, there will be no 490 acres of that fine island unoccupied.

Besides this there are of flats wholly unimproved . . . . . 440 acres.
And of flats already enclosed . . . . 103 " ·
Making a total, ultimately available of . . . . 1,033 "

The President of the Water Board puts in here Breed's Island, 720 acres, which I leave out of my calculation, although he says it is to be ultimately occupied.

The filled area of South Boston (not including streets and
    squares) is about . . . . 675 acres.
Of this, there are built upon and improved . . . . 285 "
Leaving of available unimproved land . . . . 390 "

I am not overstating it, therefore, when I say that South Boston itself is not half full.

The area of the flats on the northerly shore, which may be
    added, is about . . . . 600 acres.

The Commonwealth is now moving to fill up these flats, and I believe the only question is, whether it will do to fill them now, lest they get more land than can be sold.

The area of Roxbury (not including streets and squares)
    is about . . . . 2,184 acres.
Of this, there are built upon or improved . . . . 684 "
Leaving of available unimproved land about . . . . . . 1,500 "

"The foregoing estimate of the area built upon is, of course, very rough; for in cases where, to a single house, there appear upon the map to be several acres, there has been allowed to such isolated house a half acre as improved land, calling the balance unimproved.

" Besides the above 1,500 acres, there are of marsh land or flats, to be improved, 300 acres, making a total of 1,800 acres " of available unimproved land in Roxbury.

By this report Boston had, after annexing Roxbury : —

In Boston proper improved 630 acres, unimproved 340 acres.

East Boston	"	170	"	"	1,033	"
South Boston,	"	285	"	"	990	"
Roxbury,	"	684	"	"	1,800	"
Total	"	1,769	"	"	4,163	"

Of the unimproved 2,720 acres is upland, and 1,443 is marsh or flats.

This report was signed by John II. Thorndike, the President of the Cochituate Water Board, and he adds this remark : —

"When the whole territory within the present limits of Boston is peopled as densely as the portions now built upon, our population will amount to near 600,000.

"The present population of Roxbury is said to be about 30,000, and the rate of increase, for the ten years from 1855 to 1865, was nearly fifty-four per cent. ; and, upon the same basis that Boston can accommodate 600,000, Roxbury can accommodate about 400,000."

They talk about the increase of Roxbury resulting from annexation ; but we find by the best authority, — the census, which is quoted here, — that the increase of Roxbury, in population, for ten years preceding annexation, was fifty-four per cent., while that of Boston was a little over twenty-eight per cent.

Now, Mr. Chairman and gentlemen, the city of Boston has, to-day, territory sufficient to afford ample accommodations for 1,000,000 of people ; and she has to-day, including Roxbury, but 240,000.

Gentlemen may say that this land is not all filled, that it is not all adapted to building purposes, or for dwellings.   In answer to that, I have to say, that when a great city becomes crowded, she will not leave her unoccupied territory without the necessary improvements for the accommodation of her people. The Back Bay is an example.

I have a word to say with reference to this question of expansion. Gentlemen seem to have the idea that it is necessary for Boston to engross within herself the growth of the Commonwealth. It seems to be considered, for some reason, I know not what [it has figured on the reports, it is hinted here], that it is necessary for Boston to control the people who now reside within her limits, and also the growth of the Commonwealth, which happens to centre near her borders. Why? is the question; and you will find no answer. Is the growth of the Commonwealth, in wealth or population, one dollar or one person less, because people happen to live upon the hill-sides of Dorchester as a separate municipality? Is the population of the State one single person less than it would be if Boston extended her arm of protection around those citizens?

I have said that the same plea was made before this Legislature, in 1867, in reference to the annexation of Roxbury; and it is claimed that the results of the annexation of Roxbury have been such that this committee ought to be satisfied that it is for the interests of Dorchester to be annexed also. But that experiment has not been fully tried. The experiment may work well; but we say that the city of Roxbury, at the time, extended its arm across the neck, and joined hands with the city of Boston. They were really interwoven as one city. There were no natural boundaries between them. Washington Street extended entirely through both cities. There is an entire difference between that territory and Dorchester. That annexation was advantageous to Roxbury I do not deny, for I do not know; but the reason that applied in the case of Roxbury will fail utterly when applied to Dorchester.

FOREIGN INFLUENCE.

"But," says some witness, "we must be saved from the foreign element!" "The country," says Mr. Crane, "must come in and save the city. We must be saved from foreign influence." Let us see how he is going to succeed by the method of annexation.

We turn to the census of 1865, and we find that the whole population of Boston was 192,318, and her foreign population, 65,886, or thirty-four and twenty-five hundredths per cent. They annexed Roxbury, with a population of 28,426, and 9,664 foreigners, and they got thirty-four and thirty-five hundredths per cent. of the foreign element. That did not reduce it *much*. That is not the little leaven that leavens the whole lump. Now. they propose to take Dorchester which has a foreign element of twenty-one and sixty-eight hundredths per cent. ; we put Dorchester and the two cities together, and we produce this wonderfully satisfactory result : we reduce the foreign element, in this combined city of three separate municipalities, from thirty-four and thirty-five hundredths per cent. to thirty-three and sixty-five hundredths per cent., — a fact which perhaps you will be content to take as of some consequence when they talk about saving Boston from the foreign element.

Now I will take the territory which my brother Train intends to get into the city of Boston, and we will see how perfectly he will neutralize the foreign element. He has Roxbury, with thirty-four and thirty-five hundredths per cent. of foreign population ; he wants to take Dorchester, with twenty-one and sixty-eight hundredths per cent. ; Brookline, with thirty-two per cent. ; West Roxbury, with twenty-seven per cent. ; Brighton, with twenty-six per cent. ; Cambridge, with twenty-eight per cent. ; Charlestown, with twenty-three per cent. ; Somerville, with twenty-four per cent. ; Chelsea, with twenty per cent. ; North Chelsea, with sixteen per cent. ; and Winthrop, with twenty-seven per cent. I tell you, Mr.

Chairman, you have got to take a large slice of the Commonwealth to reduce the foreign element very much, especially when you select a portion of the Commonwealth that is almost as densely populated with foreigners as Boston itself.

One thing more, gentlemen, in regard to the middling classes. It is said we must keep the middling classes in Boston. By the census of May 1st, 1867, taken by the authorities of the city of Boston before the annexation of Roxbury, it appears that there were 19,000 dwelling-houses in the city of Boston. Of this number, 14,000 were of a value less than $7,000, and the greater portion between 1,000 and 3,000 dollars in value. It is said the middling classes will move out into the country, and yet you have only about 5,000 dwelling-houses in Boston owned, at least occupied, by the wealthy classes. I think this proves that there is some fallacy in these statements which are thrown round in the community to influence those persons who have not reflected on the subject.

In the report of these able Commissioners, — and I suppose my brother Train will not be offended if I also refer to the *intelligent committee of the citizens of Dorchester*, who had some interest in getting up that report, — they say, " The money invested in building up compact villages in the near suburbs should be applied within the limits of the city, thus retaining the population and wealth now lost, and adding to its character, wealth, numbers, and virtue." They say this capital ought to be kept in the city. How are you going to do it? By reaching out and taking in all the country around. That keeps the people in the city itself; but is there any change in population, so far as the Commonwealth is concerned? " But," says Mr. Crane, or somebody else, " a man wants to vote where he lives, and live where he votes." If you apply that rule, you will have to extend the limits of Boston into all those fair towns within a radius of twenty-five miles of Boston.

It is said that Boston is now growing towards the south;

that the tendency of growth is in that direction. I deny the
proposition. It is a fallacy. Boston grows within her own
limits towards her southern border, and why? Because there
is cheap, unoccupied land. South Boston is not half occupied. Washington Village is in its embryo state, with much
vacant land. The city of Boston, within the last three years,
has simply changed the centre of her business. She is growing, within her own limits, towards the south; but let us see
whether or not the town of Dorchester has been growing
more rapidly than other regions around Boston. I deny the
proposition that the tendency is into the country south of
the city. I admit that the growth of Boston is in the direction of the Back Bay; but it is because the city is filling up
her own territory, within her own limits. She has not
"slopped over" very badly, as yet, into the town of Dorchester. In Somerville, there were built, in 1867 and 1868, 600
dwelling-houses. In Cambridge, last year, there were erected
595 buildings, mostly houses. A late paper reports 500
transactions in real estate in Newton in 1868. The little
town of Winchester, eight miles from Boston, has increased
its population, in 1867 and 1868, from 466 polls to 630
polls, — an increase of between thirty and forty per cent. ;
showing, Mr. Chairman, that the growth outside of Boston
is not confined to the southern side, but extends everywhere.
It extends all around us; it extends wherever facilities are
offered for travel, for the comforts of home, for the education
of children, and where the country is healthful and agreeable.
It is not, then, as has been stated, tending more outwards
towards the south than it is outwards to the north or to the
west.

Lest I weary the committee with these details, I must
hasten forward to other matters.

It has been said here that the people would not leave the
city of Boston if they could get cheap land within its limits.
Well, sir, all I know about that is, that there is a good deal
of pretty cheap land in Boston. It is within reach, very ac-

cessible, and yet the people of Boston do not build on it, but they go ten miles beyond, and build up the beautiful, thriving towns throughout the Commonwealth ; why should they not?

But, say this learned Commission, we should retain the capital which now goes in millions to build up Chicago and New York and the great cities of the West ; we should keep it here. Let us have their precise words, because the announcement is very remarkable, and to me exceedingly interesting : " The amount of Boston capital invested in real estate in the cities of New York and Chicago, not to mention numerous other localities, is estimated to reach millions of dollars. This capital should be employed here, but will not be, so long as Boston maintains its present contracted limits." No ; nor while grass grows, or water runs. The wealth which has built up Lowell and Lawrence, the wealth which opens the mines of Pennsylvania and the mines of Colorado, should be employed here, in building up Washington Village and Dorchester! It is not right that this wealth should go out and build up there faster than it could here! I say, Mr. Chairman and gentleman, that every man in Massachusetts ought to be proud that it is so. Better that it should go out to build up cities and towns, to open ways of communication across the continent, than that it should be retained here to build up a single city. Better for the honor and fame of Boston and Massachusetts, that Boston should send her capital forth to civilize, enlighten, and educate the world than that she should sit supreme upon a few hills, and reign over a single port. If there is anything of which Massachusetts is proud, it is of the influence which has gone from her through the continent, elevating races, building up cities and towns, and spreading the institutions of religion and learning.

There are some minor considerations which, perhaps, I may pass over with a comment or two.

You are told the post-office facilities out in Dorchester are not in all respects what they should be ; but I apprehend you will not destroy the town of Dorchester to give my friend Pierce here a penny-post to his chocolate mills ; and I don't believe he would ask it.

Then the town house is too small, or the town meeting is too large. That is a matter of very little consequence, for the people of Dorchester can have just such a town house as they please.

But something has been said about the water front. Will annexation, Mr. Chairman, make commerce upon a water front which has been a failure for a hundred years? Will it make Dorchester a great port of entry? Will it call into requisition any portion of Neponset River? Will it build up Dorchester Bay? Annexation, pure and simple? What has the city of Boston to do with all these enterprises? It is private enterprise, private capital, influenced and stimulated by the demands of commerce, which should build up these sea-walls, and docks, and wharves, all along from Neponset River to South Boston Point. It is not annexation, but private enterprise, stimulated by the demands of commerce.

I leave this subject, gentlemen, as a humbug, and one which has no foundation, and no reality whatsoever.

COMMERCE.

I come now to another point, which is of some consequence in the consideration of this matter, — the commerce of Boston. It is said annexation is to increase the commerce of Boston, and improve her commercial position. I deny that proposition, and call for proof. Does the commerce of Boston depend upon the ability of the people, who happen to reside within a certain limited circle, to consume the commodities with which commerce deals? Is that what makes commerce flourish? Does the commerce of Boston depend upon so frail a staff as the contributions of Massachusetts alone? California has more to do with the commerce of the city of Boston, than three-quarters, yes, than all the towns in the

5

Commonwealth. Cold and frigid Alaska has much more to promise the commerce of Boston than a dozen Dorchesters. The commerce of Boston is dependent for its prosperity upon the business of the broad continent, and it cannot be that annexation will have the slightest influence.

How stands the commerce of Boston to-day? It is said that this measure will increase the commercial facilities of Boston. I beg leave to call upon Mr. Loring, who has testified upon this subject with a fairness and candor which have not been surpassed by anybody who has testified upon either side. He tells you that at East Boston there is room and to spare for the commerce of the city ; that the wharves do not pay interest; that his own wharves lie languishing. East Boston looks across the water, and begs for that flow of population and that flow of commerce which is to build her up. Her buildings stand unoccupied; her wharves do not pay dividends. Go up to Charlestown ; go around all the sinuosities of the harbor, and you will find that the wharves which, in years gone by, paid the best interest, are now either silent and utterly unoccupied, or partially so. Mr. Loring tells us that the commercial facilities of Boston to-day are greater by far than the wants of Boston can be for many years to come, judging from her present growth. I think there is nobody here to controvert that testimony ; and Mr. Crane came to the aid of Mr. Loring, for he testified that the commerce of Boston was not equal to the facilities for commerce which Boston possessed. How, then, about those magnificent structures at those remote points, the Lord knows where, away out by Mr. Preston's chocolate mill? Annexation to change it ! It is true that the same amount of business may be done now at the wharves of Boston in much less space than the same business could have been done in years ago, by reason of the better facilities for loading and unloading, and the use of steamboats and vessels of larger tonnage than formerly.

But, Mr. Chairman and gentlemen, when we are told that

something must be done to increase the commerce and commercial position of Boston, let us look it squarely in the face, and see if annexation is the remedy. No, gentlemen, I know it is not, and you know it is not. I have referred to the testimony of Mr. Crane. I admire Mr. Crane. He is a man who ought to be encouraged and maintained. He is a man of progress. He is a man of ideas. He is one of the men who help to advance the civilization of the world. But I submit to you that his flights were exceedingly high. He occasionally lights upon the solid earth, and he did so here. He comes out and declares that *cheap transportation will save Boston.* Thank you, Mr. Crane! Cheap transportation will save Boston. That is precisely the point. This fathoms the whole subject. Not annexation, not a little piece of Dorchester, nor the whole of it, nor yet of all this magic circle of towns about which my brother Train talks. Cheap transportation! That is the point exactly. All understand it; and at the other end of the capitol, tonight, I doubt not, the walls echo and re-echo with the declaration that "cheap transportation will save Boston," — for that I understand to be the burden of the speech which is to be delivered there this evening by Mr. Crane.

I say, then, to those gentlemen, who want to spend money in grand hotel enterprises upon high hills, "Instead of annexing the territory of Dorchester in the hope to increase the commerce and raise the commercial rank of Boston, spend a little money in sending steamboats to the great ports of the world; support those lines against disaster and misadventure, until they maintain themselves. Extend the lines of railroad from tide water at Boston backward to the lakes, westward to the prairies, and southward to the gulf. Bring your harbor, bring your city, within cheap and easy communication with the great granaries of the world, and you have accomplished that which will make the commerce of Boston equal that of 'Liverpool.' When you have done these things, you may talk about Boston as 'the Liverpool of America.'"

But they knew that this point was weak, Mr. Chairman and gentlemen. It is in the report, and it is out of the report. It is not quite in, and it is not quite out. It is not quite in the testimony, and not quite out. It is in just enough to talk about, and not quite enough to swear by. Who is there who says that the commerce of Boston is to be benefited to the extent of a single dollar by this proposition of annexation? Not a soul dares testify to it, and their own witness denies it. Mr. Quincy, a man who is heir to love and veneration for the city of Boston, the second mayor of the Quincy race, a man who knows the history and the progress, and the wants of Boston, and represents them as well as any man alive, comes in to-day and tells you that he cannot see, for his life, wherein this annexation of territory can benefit Boston in her commerce, or in any other way.

I say, then, to our friends, build your steamboats and your railroads, and then issue grand hotel circulars, and talk about finding a man in the country to pay $120,000 interest for a hotel on the top of a hill in Dorchester.

Another reason which is assigned, and, in my judgment, the only real one, is that real estate in Dorchester will rise in value by annexation. Remember, Mr. Chairman and gentlemen (for let us consider these things fairly, as they put them), remember that annexation is to be sought for the purpose of securing cheap land for the middle classes. And there it is, — cheap land and beautiful as lies beneath the broad sun, that any man can buy who wants to ; and yet our friends want to annex it to Boston, in the first place, so as to stimulate the price, — all for the good of the middle classes ! I do not like to use the phrase "land speculation" in connection with this matter. I should be very sorry if any person should imagine that I believe any one of the gentlemen who embark in this hotel enterprise, — which I do not mean to condemn or make any fun of, except so far as reading* the document may be ludicrous, — do so with any view to a land speculation. I do not mean to intimate, gentlemen, that such a man as Mr. Tileston, than whom there is probably no more honorable man in the Commonwealth, would engage deliberately in an absolute land speculation, for the purpose of putting money into his own pocket. But, gentlemen, they want to raise the price of land. They come in here and ask you, as members of the Legislature, to grant them annexation to raise the price of land. What great blessing is that to the people of Dorchester? I do not quite see it. I understand that not half the people of Dorchester own any land at all. The few gentlemen who happen to own the territory of Dorchester are getting a direct advantage of the rise of the land, and everybody else a direct disadvantage. The laboring man, the man who hires his dwelling-house, makes no very great gain by having the taxes and rent raised.

But suppose it is all so, is this a real estate broker's shop? Are we bulls and bears, upon the one side, and upon the other bulling the market for real estate, or bearing it? Not at all. But whether it be so or not, I apprehend that that single consideration will never influence a Legislature acting for the good of the whole Commonwealth. It is of no earthly consequence, here or there, and no legislator can justify himself in taking that position.

The water argument cannot be used here, for the President of the Water Works declares that the capacity of the works will be exhausted in five years. And yet, John Preston wants a pipe to Commercial Point!

I say, that while one portion of the population of Dorchester would be benefited, another portion would be injured by the mere change in the price of land. I say to you further, Mr. Chairman, that you can well afford to let the increase of Dorchester be governed by the common and ordinary laws governing population. It need not be stimulated, it ought not to be stimulated, by any act of legislation. I will not deny that you may, by your action, inflate the price of land in Dorchester; but this broad earth is yet large enough for all its people, and if you bring the tide of population out to the lands of Dorchester (and I admit that population is very likely to go where real estate is rising in price), the compensation is to be found somewhere. Boston grows beyond the natural law of demand and supply, some other place falls behind; or, if it does not actually fall behind, fails to keep up in the march of progress.

I have a few more comments upon these various reasons which have been given. A park is wanted, it is said, — a park of 800 acres. Our good friend, Mr. Tileston, one of the most noble-souled men in all the world, wants to see a park down in Mattapan; and, pointing with his cane, he says, "Here is a beautiful place for a park, out in Mattapan. Just look at it! You can buy it cheap!" Exactly so. But is Boston suffering for a park? "Oh, but New York has a park; other cities have parks." Boston has a park, which is not yet rivalled by any city on this continent. New York has a park; but New York is a city of brick and stone from the Battery to the gates of the Central Park. The Common and the Public Garden are said to be the lungs of Boston. New York has no such lungs. Surrounded as she is on three sides by water, the country cannot come down to meet her, and she has a park, a beautiful and grand one. Nobody can object to it. It is an honor to New York. But how is it with Boston? Why, gentlemen, Boston is surrounded and embraced by a park more beautiful than Central Park, ten thousand times over. The grand park which surrounds and embraces the city of Boston is covered all over with the evidences of art and taste, — fine streets, fine avenues, beautiful residences, grand gardens; variety, beauty, everywhere. This is the grand park, the Central Park of the city of Boston. I do not believe that the child is yet born who will see Mattapan converted into a park for the city of Boston. The same idea is embraced, I see, in the circular setting forth the grand hotel scheme: "By aiding in the erection of the grand hotel, the citizens of Dorchester will not aid themselves, but help to preserve their territory to be made a part of Boston, — the Central Park of the metropolis of New England." I think, gentlemen, that this park may be left to grow something besides flowers at present. Central Park of New York, as compared with that of Boston, is like a single solitary, beautiful acre, and no more.

Now, they say the people want it. That is one of the last things, I suppose, we shall hear: "The people of Dorchester want annexation." Well, some of them do, and some of them do not; and some who did, now do not. That is the fact about it. But it is not a question whether the people want it; it is a question of high state polity; it is a question affecting the whole Commonwealth. You are not, therefore, to be led captive by the idea (I know, gentlemen, that there is no danger) that the people of Boston, or the people of Dorchester, or of the suburbs of Boston, have a right to take the destiny of the Commonwealth within their own grasp. You have something to say upon that subject.

Now, Mr. Chairman, I have to submit that these are the reasons, and all the reasons, which have been urged, in print or by testimony, before this committee, or in this capitol this year, upon the subject of annexation. I may not have elaborated them, as my friend Train will, but I believe I have touched every one of them, as they lie embodied in the reports, or as they have been stated in the testimony. But are there no objections to this grand scheme of annexation? I have adverted to the loss that Norfolk county will suffer; I have adverted to the fact that one-third the population and one-half the wealth of the Commonwealth will be concentrated under one city government. I do not especially represent the people of Dorchester here, but I beg leave to call your attention, in a very few words, to the change which will take place in their relations upon the subject of debt.

DEBT.

The valuation of Boston last year was	$493,573,700
" " Dorchester last year was	15,326,300
Total valuation,	$508,900,000

City net debt of Boston, April 1st, 1869, by auditor's report, $13,824,653
Debt of Dochester, report of 1869, 36,607

Aggregate debt of Boston and Dorchester, §13,861,260

Dorchester's proportion of the aggregate debt, $\frac{15.326.300}{508.900.000}$
of 13,861,260, is $417,453
Deduct her present debt, 36,607

Showing an increase of indebtedness of $380,846
to be assumed and paid by Dorchester in case of annexation.

But if Mayor Shurtleff's estimate that two-thirds of the sum
appropriated last year for betterments will be returned
to the treasury, which is undoubtedly too liberal, an
estimate then of the actual debt of Boston now is §11,780,987
Add debt of Dorchester as before, 36,607

Aggregate debt of Boston and Dorchester, §11,817,694

Dorchester's proportion of the aggregate debt, $\frac{15.326.300}{508.900.000}$
of 11,817,694, is §355,907
Deduct present debt of Dorchester, . 36,607

Showing an increase of indebtedness of $319,300
to be assumed and paid by Dorchester in case of annexation.

INTEREST.

The total amount of interest, premium, etc., paid by Boston
for the financial year, ending April 1, 1868, vide page 11,
city auditor's report, was $1,277,278

This includes water-debt interest of §515,245 (vide city aud.
rep., page 124), but as the Water Works yielded an in-
come of §551,839
(vide aud. rep., page 13), and caused an expense
to the city of §148,462

(vide aud. rep., page 124), the balance $403,377

Should be deducted from the total amount,
leaving $873,901
There should also be deducted for interest re-
ceived (vide aud. rep., page 13), two items
of interest §175,929
77,626
$253,555

Leaving net interest, premium, etc., $620,346

This is upon an indebtedness of	$8,947,530
(*vide* city aud. rep., page 18).	
But the present net city debt of Boston is	$13,824,653
(*vide* aud. rep., of April 1, 1869).	
And the interest account must be proportionately increased, making the interest account for 1869,	$958,484
To which add three per cent. of indebtedness required to be raised by taxation for sinking fund (*vide* city aud. rep., page 246),	414,739
	$1,373.223
To be raised by taxation this year for interest of the old debt of Boston.	
To this add interest on the debt of Dorchester, $36,607 at eight per cent.,	2,928
Making an amount of	$1,376,151
To be raised by taxation for interest, etc., on the aggregate debt of Boston and Dorchester.	
The valuation of Boston last year was	$493,573,700
" " Dorchester "	15,326,300
Aggregate valuation of Boston and Dorchester,	$508,900,000
Dorchester's proportion of this interest will be $\frac{15,326,300}{508,900,000}$ of $1,376,151,	$41,444
Deduct interest on Dorchester's debt,	2,928
Making	$38,516

*To be assumed and paid by Dorchester each year upon the old debt of Boston.

---

* The auditor's report, to whose pages reference is made, is the report of 1868. The report for 1869 is not yet published, but the figures of April 1, 1869, used here, were furnished by the city auditor.

It is sometimes claimed that the water debt of Boston will extinguish itself by receipts from the water rates, and ought not to be reckoned as a part of the city debt. How far this is true, appears from the auditor's report of 1868, as follows : —

Interest paid on the water debt,	$515,245
Expenses of the Water Board,	148,462
Total expenditures,	$663,707
Receipts from water rates,	551,839
Balance of expenditures over receipts,	$111,868

Showing that the water works are actually *increasing* the city debt at the rate of over $100,000 a year. The Chestnut Hill Reservoir is *not* included in this statement.

I do not see any escape from those figures. I have tried to be entirely fair in this matter. If I am wrong, I hope I shall be put right. Dorchester is left to raise the beautiful little sum of $38,516 annually, as her contribution towards the payment of interest on the debt of the city of Boston. I do not believe this matter has been carefully investigated. The people of Dorchester cannot be aware that they are to take upon their own shoulders $355,000 of indebtedness, for which they must be responsible, and a present interest of $38,000 annually, and with a prospect of an increase in the future.

These are some of the objections which may be urged. There are many others; but I say now, — coming to the last subject to which I shall have the honor to refer, — that this whole scheme is contrary to the public policy of this Commonwealth. I stand here, Mr. Chairman and gentlemen, and claim, I believe, with very good reason, that neither of the petitioners, neither the city of Boston nor the town of Dorchester, have made a case upon a single one of the propositions. Gentlemen may say to you, "Oh, well, if we have not made out a good case upon any one of the propositions, yet upon the whole we may have done so. I was taught, early in my study of the law, that when you undertake to establish an affirmative proposition by many facts, every link in the chain of evidence must be fairly proved; any link not being proved, the conclusion fails. I do not understand how you can make a good case out of a number of propositions together, each of which has, separately, utterly and totally failed. I cannot understand how you can make out any case for annexation upon the general, broad whole, when every one of the single propositions has utterly and totally failed, and even been abandoned in the presence of the committee. Sewerage, harbor improvements, schools, sidewalks, police, everything has failed, and yet you may be asked to come in and say that, upon the whole, **the annexation scheme has not failed. .**

I undertake now to say that this scheme is contrary to the public policy of this Commonwealth. I may be wearying the committee, but perhaps they will bear with me while I read a few extracts upon this question. I know this is elementary, and you may think it unnecessary that I should spend my time and yours in attempting to prove to you that which is elementary, a matter of history, and to which every man in the Commonwealth will say "Yes;" but it seems to me that in a matter of this consequence I am justified in asking your attention to a few general propositions.

I have shown you that it is proposed to put one-third the population and one-half the wealth of the State under the control of the city of Boston. My brother Train cannot escape from this. Although the record says, "the annexation of Dorchester," yet he says, and his clients are saying, "not Dorchester alone. We must have a magnificent, grand metropolis, including all the towns in the neighborhood of Boston." I argue the whole question. I say, before you take the first step upon the journey towards this consolidation of wealth and power, you will be recreant to your duty to the Commonwealth, unless you determine the question whether it is in accordance with the policy of the Commonwealth to build up great, overwhelming corporations like this which is proposed. Let this scheme be accomplished, and how soon will you have the City Hall rivalling in power the State House itself? Go on with your schemes of annexation, and the City Hall rules Massachusetts. His Excellency the Governor sinks into insignificance in the presence of the Chief Magistrate of the city. To-day, Mr. Chairman and gentlemen, — I wish to impress it upon you, — to-day the disbursements of the city of Boston, the patronage and power of Boston, by her money, exceed that of the State. The treasury of the city of Boston wields more patronage and power than that of this Commonwealth. If you grant the prayer of these petitioners, you are entering upon a course not in harmony with the general spirit of our government. The treasury of the Commonwealth, gentlemen, with a city like this, united in interest, united in power, and all her representatives acting together in the Legislature as one solid phalanx, — the treasury of the State becomes simply the treasury of the city. Are you prepared for this? Who will deny the proposition? Boston, when she knocks at the door of the Legislature, is always heard. I am not one of that class of men who love to rail against the power of Boston, and I would not have you understand that I would join in that clamor which is sometimes raised, that Boston rules the State. I do not believe in it. Boston has her proper and just influence upon the great interests of the Commonwealth. Boston has intelligence, and wealth, and public spirit, and a thousand other things which fit her for high positions in government; but Boston never, in my judgment, should reach the position where she will have it in her power to dictate the policy of the State.

New York rules the Empire State; and you propose, here in this Commonwealth of Massachusetts, to erect one single corporation greater really in strength and power than the balance of the State itself; not by the annexation of Dorchester alone, but by what is to follow. New York is able to transfer her Mayor to the Chief Executive Chair, in spite of the votes of, and in opposition to, the political sentiment of a vast majority of the people of that great State outside of the city. Do you want to extend this evil? Mr. Quincy comes in here and tells you, that, in his judgment, such great municipal corporations are a misfortune, a calamity to the State. You, Mr. Chairman and gentlemen, must consider this question and determine it, before you take this new departure upon this road towards consolidation. Now is the time to settle it. If you do not settle it now, the day has passed by, and Massachusetts surrenders herself to Boston.

You may think me somewhat enthusiastic in this portion of my argument. I simply say, that when you consolidate so many municipalities in one, you make their interests identical upon some points. Whenever the interests of Boston are in controversy, — her real or imaginary interests, — every one of her representatives, coming from any portion of her wide territory, will hold up the flag of Boston, and will fight under it in the halls of legislation. Now they divide, they do not all concentrate together.

In this connection, permit me to read a few short extracts from the first volume of De Tocqueville's "Democracy in America," — a work which has become an accredited authority on the subject of American institutions : —

"The American Revolution broke out, and the doctrine of the sovereignty of the people came out of the townships, and took possession of the State. Every class was enlisted in its cause; battles were fought and victories obtained for it; it became the law of laws." — (p. 70.)

"Town-meetings are to liberty what primary schools are to science; they bring it within the people's reach; they teach men how to use, and how to enjoy it. A nation may establish a free government; but without municipal institutions, it cannot have the spirit of liberty." — (p. 76.)

" The township, taken as a whole, and in relation to the central government, is only an individual, like any other to whom the theory I have just described is applicable. Municipal independence in the United States is, therefore, a natural consequence of this very principle of the sovereignty of the people. All the American republics recognize it more or less; but circumstances have peculiarly favored its growth in New England." — (p. 81.)

"The native of New England is attached to his township, because it is independent and free; his co-operation in its affairs insures his attachment to its interest; the well-being it affords him secures his affection; and its welfare is the aim of his ambition and of his future exertions. He takes a part in every occurrence in the place; he practises the art of government in the small sphere within his reach; he accustoms himself to those forms without which liberty can only advance by revolutions; he imbibes their spirit; he acquires a taste for order, comprehends the balance of powers, and collects clear, practical notions on the nature of his duties and the extent of his rights." — (pp. 85, 86.)

In the "Galaxy" for the present month, there is an article on "The Great Danger of the Republic," from which I read the following passage : —

" Under a representative system, the nearer a representative is to his constituents, the more faithfully and honestly will he carry out their wishes and guard their interests. In our small States there is much greater purity in the administration of affairs than in the large States.

And experience in respect to official conduct shows, that the further power exercised by a public officer is removed from the people, the larger the constituencies, and the more remote the objects of legislation from the particular attention of the people, the more the sense of individual responsibility is lost, and the greater will be the opportunity and temptation for misrepresentation, infidelity, and corruption on the part of the representative. In small States the public officers perform their duties in the very presence and under the immediate eye of their constituents. They cannot abuse their trust without immediate exposure and dishonor. This is the chief cause of the success of the Swiss republic. And, in this particular, our government is like that of Switzerland, except that it has its foundations in the towns, a smaller political division of the country, and a most invaluable nursery of republicanism. The cantons of Switzerland correspond with our counties, and these are composed of the towns, each of which possesses considerable power of self-government in its domestic affairs. Our counties, also, exercise a large degree of local legislation and control in respect to matters of internal administration, and these counties compose the States. The strength of our system lies in this distribution of powers. The small local republics of our towns and municipalities educate our people in the principles and practice of self-government, and thus preserve among them, pure and fresh, the spirit of freedom and republicanism."

I also read the following extracts from the debates in the Constitutional Convention of 1853 : —

"I would guard, with jealous care, the independence of these local assemblies, the town meetings, which are the fairest growth of liberty, and in which the best security for its protection is to be found.

"These local, separate, and independent assemblies through which the life-blood of the national heart flows and circulates, in which matters are discussed important enough to awaken interest, but not important enough to awaken ambition, are the fountains from which our political prosperity has flowed. May they ever remain as pure as they have hitherto been. What is the primal excellence of this Commonwealth that we so honor and love? It is, that it is an aggregate, and not an interfusion, of these local communities. The several towns that make up this Commonwealth do not, like drops of water, part with their own identity to swell the general stream, but they rather blend like flowers in a garland, or stars in a constellation, each retaining its own light and its own beauty, but each contributing to the light and beauty of the whole."

Hon. George S. Hillard.

"I venture to assert that the government of cities is shown from the history of the world, to have been universally bad; but history furnishes no instance in which a government vested in the country, has ever been exercised for the oppression of the city. Never."

Hon. George S. Boutwell.

Turn where you will, among the authors who have written upon this subject, and you will find the same principles expressed. Here is a document which I found, printed, among the papers connected with the annexation of Roxbury. It is a remonstrance by George Morey and thirty-two others, among whom are the late Josiah Quincy, Sr., and John A. Andrew, in which they protest against the doctrine of consolidation, and in which the Hon. Josiah Quincy, Sr., denounces this whole subject as an abomination in his eyes.

Having gone over the ground to show you, as I think I have, that the case is not sustained on the part of the petitioners; that the various reasons given by them are not such as ought to move you to grant their prayer; and having spoken as fully as I think I ought, under all the circumstances, of the true policy of the Commonwealth in this respect, — I come now to the only remaining topic to which I think it necessary to advert. I ask you if there is not some other way to answer all the demands of the city of Boston? I am not here with any particular theory of my own, and I am not entitled to take any credit to myself for having any theory at all upon this subject, for the matter has been brought to my attention by discussion with my associates here, and with other gentlemen; and I am led to put the question to you, whether there is not another way to meet the fancied wants of the city of Boston.

If, Mr.· Chairman, there are any wants connected with the subject of sewerage; if any of the towns which drain themselves into the Charles or the Mystic, or into the Bay of Boston or Dorchester, ought to be under one jurisdiction for streets, for public highways, for sewerage, — I do not see that we are at a loss to know how to accomplish that end. What is a county? A county extends over a large number of municipalities for certain definite and fixed purposes, and the business of the county is committed to the hands of a tribunal called County Commissioners. The city of Boston has its Street Commissioners and its Harbor Commissioners, — the latter, I believe, acting under the jurisdiction of the State. Take the towns. The Selectmen take charge of the government of the town, and expend a certain amount of money in a certain direction.. They have a certain jurisdiction, the Overseers of the Poor another, the Surveyor of Highways another, the Treasurer another, and so on through the whole list. All the authority in a town is divided, and there is no one responsible head, except that from which it springs, — the people.

Now, sir, suppose you should erect a quasi county here, and should elect a board of commissioners, a portion of them to go out of office yearly; electing them for a period of time sufficiently long for them to have a plan and maintain it; electing them by districts, and giving into the hands of that central board the power to go out and provide streets and drainage for all this county, and have the direction of rivers and harbors throughout this great municipal district, — will you have anything that has not been heard of before, in this country? Will you have advanced a single step upon any new invention? I think if there is ever to be any consolidation of this immense territory under one government, it must not be one government for all purposes, but a government for those matters only which can only be answered by a union of the territory. If you desire to take from the county of Norfolk for these purposes every inch of her territory, there is nobody here to object. If you want to put Middlesex and Norfolk and Suffolk together, who can find a word of fault? Give this district as many broad avenues as she can pay for. Give to Boston and to the suburbs all the advantage of drainage which they can possibly get. By the union, put these subjects under one power.

I think, Mr. Chairman, this is a plain proposition, and one that can be appreciated by every citizen of Massachusetts. We see it in operation every day. I have broached this subject to some of our annexation friends; but I have generally found them to be wedded to their annexation scheme, and they thought I had got off into the region of wild imagination, — that the thing was too complicated. If it is more complicated than the present management at City Hall, I beg to know how. Give to this Central Board, elected by the people, perfect control over as large a metropolis as you please. Extend Boston as London has been extended. Let Boston be known, at home and abroad, if you please, as a city of a million inhabitants, and a hundred miles in area. Save us simply those rights which are in harmony with the old and well-settled policy of this Commonwealth, — the distinctive characteristic and feature of the Commonwealth. Give us those things, we will take care of our paupers, we will provide all our local charities, we will put our streets in perfect order and condition, we will take care of our schools, for Dorchester can take care of her schools as well as Boston can take care of them for her. Leave us in the enjoyment of that individuality and identity which belong to us, and you may take all those powers which simply relate to streets, drains, and those things which are for the universal public advantage. Take them all, and we shall be harmed not at all.

Here is a map of the city of London and its suburbs. The city of London proper covers but a very small space on this map; but, so far as the streets and sewers are concerned, all this territory is managed by a Board of Public Works, elected by the several municipalities. My partner has handed to the committee the law passed in 1855, making this provision. Now, I ask, Mr. Chairman and gentlemen, not that you adopt any scheme of mine, not that you step a single step in the way of reporting it; but I ask you, before you begin the process of consolidation by annexing Dorchester to Boston, and commit the Commonwealth to this daring scheme, to pause and see whether or not you cannot safely say to the Legislature at this session, that the subject of annexation has now assumed such magnitude that you feel it to be a duty to recommend the appointment of a wise and learned Commission to take this whole subject into consideration, to sit during the next recess

7

of the Legislature, and mature a plan which in their judgment will meet the wants of this community, preserving, so far as they can, the separate municipalities, and report a measure to the next Legislature. If that action is not satisfactory, and cannot be made so, we shall have the advantage of an investigation which is not partisan in its character; an investigation which will be deliberate, cool, and careful; a Commission appointed to act for the interest of the State as well as for the interests of the people of Dorchester or Boston.

I submit, Mr. Chairman and gentlemen, whether it would not be quite as wise, when we are embarking upon a new and great enterprise, to give the people of the Commonwealth time to consider whether this, the first step, shall be taken. Take the first step, and it can never be recalled. If it is a wise step, a proper measure, and there are reasons for it which satisfy your minds, or can satisfy the minds of a wise Legislature, any objections must give way. But I believe, and I think, gentlemen, you must in some respects sympathize with me in that belief, that, as we stand to-day, the friends of annexation have failed utterly to prove that necessity or that great public emergency which can justify the commencement of a process by which a corporation is to be erected which shall control forever after the policy of the State. Carry out this policy, and New Bedford may take the towns around her; Taunton may step in and say, " I want to be a great city, and I will take everything there is here;" then will come Springfield, and say she is in the western part of the State, and she will take within her limits all there is up to the New York line; and Worcester will come in and say, she is the heart of the Commonwealth, and she will take the balance. Begin here, and you may as well partition out the old State between the cities; let them erect their independent governments and manage the thing as a confederacy of independent cities. Begin the process here, and Worcester and Springfield may, with the same propriety, ask an extension of their borders for the very same reasons that have been given here.

Mr. Chairman and gentlemen, I owe you an apology for having trespassed so long upon your time. I did not intend to occupy so much of it. I can only excuse myself by saying that I have felt it my duty to touch upon the various topics which have fallen under observation. I thank you very heartily for having given me so patient an audience.